Madison Square Garden: The History c
Arena

By Charles River

Andrés Nieto Porras' picture of Madison Square Garden

About Charles River Editors

Introduction

Madison Square Garden

"To think that a once scrawny boy from Austria could grow up to become Governor of the State of California and stand here in Madison Square Garden to speak on behalf of the President of the United States, that is an immigrant's dream. It is the American dream." – Arnold Schwarzenegger

Of all the great cities in the world, few personify their country like New York City. As America's largest city and best known immigration gateway into the country, the Big Apple represents the beauty, diversity and sheer strength of the United States, a global financial center that has enticed people chasing the "American Dream" for centuries.

As such, it's only fitting that Madison Square Garden, the stadium that bills itself as the world's most famous arena, resides in the heart of Manhattan. Just blocks away from the Empire State Building and situated atop Penn Station, the Garden is always bustling, whether it's for special events or as the home of the NBA's New York Knicks and NHL's New York Rangers, and all the while, performing in the Garden has been a career benchmark for artists as varied as

Elvis Presley, The Doors, Led Zeppelin, and Michael Jackson. As Billie Joel put it, "Madison Square Garden is the center of the universe as far as I'm concerned. It has the best acoustics, the best audiences, the best reputation, and the best history of great artists who have played there. It is the iconic, holy temple of Rock and Roll for most touring acts and, being a New Yorker, it holds a special significance to me."

The Garden is now nearly 50 years old, making it one of the oldest sporting venues used in professional sports, but the current arena was not the first Madison Square Garden, and the area has a history as an entertainment center dating back to the 19th century. Ironically, its location on the less crowded fringes of Manhattan in the 19th century helped establish it as a place for hucksters like P.T. Barnum to hold events. In fact, a previous Garden was one of New York City's tallest buildings in the early 20th century, and it was bankrolled by business titans like J.P. Morgan and Andrew Carnegie.

Madison Square Garden: The History of New York City's Most Famous Arena chronicles the history of one of New York's most iconic landmarks. Along with pictures of important people, places, and events, you will learn about MSG like never before, in no time at all.

Madison Square Garden: The History of New York City's Most Famous Arena

About Charles River Editors

Introduction

Chapter 1: To Delight the People of New York

"P. T. Barnum, the famous old showman, conceived the original idea of the old Garden, and now, Ringling, his successor, is vitally a part of the new Garden. … It is difficult even to imagine the day when Madison Square Park was the Potter's Field of New York, selected because it was an undesirable tract, way up in the country and out of the way. Years later, after the Square had been parked, it became the exclusive residential section of the city — the mecca of the Madisons, Van Rensselaers, and Astors, who controlled the socially elite set of the city." L.E. Curtis, author of "Madison Square Garden's Major Role in the Life and Traditions of New York City"

As is so often the case with war, the years following the American Civil War were ones of fervor and expansion, especially in the triumphant North, where celebrations of life and victory evolved into a new interest in sporting events and other forms of entertainment. That is part of the reason the first of four Madison Square Gardens came into existence.

In 1871, railroad mogul Cornelius Vanderbilt moved his terminal from New York's popular Madison Square Park to the newly completed Grand Central Terminal, which left the original building, already a popular hot spot, open to other uses. Located on a large corner lot where Fifth and Madison Avenues met with Twenty-Sixth and Twenty-Seventh Streets, the only thing keeping the area from reaching its full potential was the old train yard Vanderbilt had left behind.

Vanderbilt

This provided an opportunity for one of the 19th century's most notorious opportunists, Phineas Taylor Barnum. In April 1871, Barnum's Grand Traveling Museum, Menagerie, Caravan, and Circus debuted in Brooklyn. The show was performed under canvas tents, filling three acres of land, and it was the largest circus ever seen in the U.S. Looking for a new home for his expanding circus, he bought the lot in 1873 and started building what he originally called The Great Roman Hippodrome. L.E. Curtis explained, "For many years after 1831, the northeast corner of the Square was the passenger station of the New York and Harlem Railway. After it was abandoned by the Railroad, the property remained idle for a few seasons, until in 1873, P. T. Barnum, the famous showman, seized upon the opportunity of erecting here a Roman Hippodrome, a plan which he had cherished for years. In order to protect the large tents, he had four walls constructed and let the big canvas, for circus atmosphere, serve as a roof. Here he came on his annual pilgrimages each season to delight the people of New York with the wildest animals, the most daring and dazzling feats, the tiniest, the tallest, the fattest, and the leanest curiosities he could recruit."

Barnum

When it opened on April 27, 1874, it was little more than a large, three storied brick building with a 274-foot oval shaped arena inside. In fact, it was less than a completed building because its only roof was a circus tent that was spread over it in rainy weather. One London newspaper observed in 1873, "New York has had a real sensation in the world of amusement. The Great Roman Hippodrome which Barnum announced some time ago is completed and opened. A private rehearsal has just taken place, attended only by about 6,000 people, but to which at least 50,000 desired to be admitted. The scheme is founded on the well-established fact that the Americans like big things, and to borrow the forcible if not fascinating language of Barnum, this is the biggest thing on earth. Its seating capacity is stated to be 12,000. The track, laid out in an ellipse, is one-fifth of a mile in length. Rising nearly twenty feet all round it are the seats for the spectators, divided by grades of upholstery into gallery, dress circle, paraquet, &c. Filled as it was by an assemblage of 10,000 or 12,000 persons, and brilliantly lit by hundreds of gas-jets, the scene is one of uncommon interest and beauty."

According to an 1874 article referring to "The Great Roman Hippodrome," "Mr. Barnum seems to have devoted years to perfecting this great enterprise, and nearly one year of his personal attention was paid to it in Europe. At an expense of several hundred thousand dollars he erected a great hippodrome building in the heart of New York City, and under an outlay of over five thousand dollars each day, he has run his establishment in New York for nearly a year."

Illustrations depicting the Hippodrome

A picture of the interior

Unfortunately, the Hippodrome did not prove profitable, so Barnum was forced to take his show back on the road. During this time, he leased the building to various other organizations, including the Westminster Kennel Club, which held its first dog show there in 1877 and continues to hold its annual events at what William Vanderbilt named "Madison Square Garden" when he bought back the lease on the property in 1879. That same year, Grover Cleveland held what would be the first of many political rallies at the Garden, while boxers and bicyclists also displayed their prowess. In fact, such was the facility's popularity in the sporting world that a cycling event added to the Olympic Games was named Madison.

Vanderbilt

An 1879 picture of Madison Square Garden

It was also used for religious meetings, flower shows and beauty contests, but like Barnum, Vanderbilt had a problem establishing its viability. This was the case until July 1882, when the famous boxer John L. Sullivan agreed to hold a boxing exhibition there. According to newspaper coverage of the event, "The match between John L. Sullivan, champion pugilist of America, and Joe Collins, or 'Tug Wilson,' as he is known in the sporting world, was fought tonight at the Madison Square Garden before 15,000 people. The fight comes just within the limits of the law, which allows men to fight with boxing gloves In public. The gloves tonight were as small as possible and covered with hard kid tightly, drawn, so that a blow from one of them was almost as severe as with a naked fist. The crowd was tremendous; fully 20,000 people were outside though many held tickets. When the first cheer went up the vast throng carried away the doors on the Fourth Avenue side and tried to rush in but the Police fought them back. There were hundreds of officers present, but they had a tough job to keep the crowd in order. As the fight progressed the spectators moved in a body to the platform that served as a ring and, carrying away the benches, would have got beyond control but for the Vigorous work of the police. Madison Square Garden is in the most respectable part of the city. The streets were crowded with men and women anxious to hear how the fight ended. NO complimentary tickets were given except two each to the six leading daily papers, and every one paid from one to two, dollars to get in, so that the money to the winner aggregates a very neat little fortune."

Sullivan

TUG WILSON,
(Joe Collins.)

Tug Wilson

Suddenly, Vanderbilt realized that the sweet science could make a sweet profit, and after that, Madison Square Garden soon became known for its high profile sporting events. Over the next four years, the Garden sold out every time Sullivan boxed there.

Barnum also returned to the Garden briefly in 1882, this time bringing Jumbo, a large elephant from the London Zoo. According to the *New York Telegram*, "Such an overwhelming business was never done by any entertainment in this city before as that of the Barnum and London combined shows at Madison Square Garden, because no other show was ever given. The receipts the first week, actually exceeded $55,000, and during the second week, the indications are that the sum received will be even greater than that; the Madison Square Garden has been too small to hold the mass of people, and, as a consequence, thousands were turned away from the doors."

Jumbo in the summer of 1882

L. E. Curtis later recalled, "During the summer months the interior was decorated to resemble a garden and here one might ponder over delicate refreshments to the lithesome refrains of a Theodore Thomas orchestra or the measured tread of a hundred-piece military band conducted by Patrick S. Gilmore. Here, in this enormous, casually developed barrack, the- great revival spectacle conducted by Moody and Sankey was held, shortly after their triumphant return from Europe in 1875. Gradually, as the importance of mass entertainments and exhibits increased, the old structure was found uncomfortably inadequate and in 1889 the first ground was broken for the new three-million dollar structure."

Chapter 2: Time and Tradition

"Cities throughout the world are famous for the structures which time and tradition have made a part of their life and history. Rome with her crumbling Colosseum, Paris dominated o'er by the gigantic Eiffel Tower, London with the gay and sparkling Covent Garden, are synonymous. The Leaning Tower of Pisa is more noted than the city of its site. In many respects Madison Square Garden and New York are the New World examples of traditional land marks. The mere mention of Madison Square Garden in any cosmopolitan city of the world is equivalent to referring to the metropolis of America. Such prestige and place in tradition are not merely a matter of chance or condition. There seems in every instance to have been a special background, an atmosphere pungently redolent of the past and propitiously suggestive of the greater things to come. A history of the events presided over by this Moorish mass of architecture might well be called an American epic. Primarily it was built by the people, for the people, and for over a quarter of a century, the echo of its activities made the history of American life. Here throbbed the pulse of a nation, at work as well as at play." - L. E. Curtis

In spite of the circus and sports events, it was soon clear that Madison Square Garden was not designed for long-term success. By 1888, there were too many other attractions vying for people's entertainment dollars, many of which were offering interesting events in much more comfortable surroundings. *Harper's Weekly* weighed in, saying that the Garden "has been marked these many years as the place for some building of public entertainment much finer than the present structure."

Tired of the project, Vanderbilt sold out to J.P. Morgan, who in turn ordered the brick hull torn down and hired Stanford White to construct a new Madison Square Garden in its place. However, before that began, there was one final show; as one newspaper reported in late July 1889, "The plans for the new building on the site of Madison Square Garden have been completed and made public. The work will begin about Nov, 1. Before this step toward the final breaking-up to the historic old garden is taken, however, an important event will take place there that will serve a lilting wind-up to the history of the famous resort. The American Shipping and Industrial League will hold an international maritime exhibition from Sept, 11 to Oct. 21. The mammoth h garden will be turned into an indoor ocean, with boats, launches, row boats and ship models scattered all over its watery surface. ... The great feature of the exhibition will be a canal, one-eighth of a mile long and 25 feet wide. It will cover the old track where so many pedestrians have piled up the wearily gained miles. There will be provided boats for visitors and other craft will be on exhibition. It will be quite a novel sight to see little steam launches putting about the great building, running races with single sculls, or coaxing a plodding canal boat to try a hand at a race."

Morgan

White

At the time he was commissioned to draw up plans for the new Garden, White was a partner with McKim, Mead & White, a firm that had designed some of New York's most beautiful mansions, including the Fifth Avenue homes of the Vanderbilt's and the Astor's. They had also designed the famed Washington Square Arch. In writing about White, to whom much of the credit belonged for the second Madison Square Garden's beauty, Curtis described him as "a young man of thirty-six, who had already been heralded as a great architect. To him was entrusted the commission of designing New York's great play palace. Stanford White had roved extensively and the architecture of the Old World inspired him to revive it in the New. Working with an unsuppressed freedom and colossal appeal to the people for greater appreciation of architecture, it has been said of his work that 'his buildings were seen and admired by all classes from the man in the street to the millionaire' and surely this was true of Madison Square Garden."

In fact, Curtis did not know the whole story about White. That's because in addition to designing the Garden and other similar spaces, he also designed a secret hideaway in his own home where an aspiring young dancer, Evelyn Nesbit, then 16 years old, would entertain him during sexually inappropriate meetings. This and other dalliances would later lead to one of the most notorious events in Garden history.

Nesbit

Before that all took place, the new Garden had to be completed. A July 18, 1888 article reported, "Ground will be broken in October for the mammoth amusement building to be erected on the block now occupied by Madison Square Garden. All of the stock issued by the new company amounting to $1,100,000 has been placed. The new Madison Square Garden will consist of a five-story building, and will contain a great amphitheater, where large shows may be given in the presence of 10,000 spectators, or mass meetings held."

The following month, W. A. Haines, Secretary of the Madison Square Garden Company, told a reporter, "The Madison Square Garden Company has placed all of its stock and bonds. It has made all its contracts and commenced taking down the old building, preparatory to the erection of a magnificent new structure, which will be both a benefit and an ornament to the metropolis. The list of stockholders is itself a guarantee of judicious and proper management. The building will cover the entire block, bounded by Madison and Fourth Avenues, Twenty-sixth and Twenty-seventh Streets, 200 by 425 feet. The exterior will be built of buff brick and white terra cotta, and a covered arcade will extend along the Madison Avenue front, returning 112 feet on the side street. There will also be a small arcade at the Fourth Avenue entrance to the amphitheatre. At the corner of Madison Avenue and Twenty-sixth Street a tower will rise 300 feet, with elevators and staircase, to an observation lookout 250 foot above the sidewalk. The building will be built entirely of masonry, iron and glass, and will be absolutely fireproof throughout. It will be lighted by an incandescent system of electric lighting and will be heated and ventilated in the most thorough and approved manner. The amphitheatre is approached from Madison Avenue by a central entrance twenty-four feet wide, or directly from Fourth Avenue."

As magnificent as the exterior of the building was to be, the interior was to be even more dramatic. Haines continued, "The dimensions of the amphitheatre will be 315 by 200 feet, with a track one-tenth of a mile long and a permanent seating capacity of 8,000, inclusive of upward of one hundred and fifty private boxes, and when floored over and filled with scats for conventions and similar purposes the amphitheatre will have a capacity of about twelve thousand. Special attention will be paid to its acoustic properties. Underneath the seats of the amphitheatre and sunk six feet below the street and extending around the entire amphitheatre will be a continuous hall thirty-five feet wide and twenty-two feet high in its highest part, adapted for the stabling of horses for the horse show, circus and similar purposes, or for exhibitions. This space is perfectly lighted by windows opening directly on the street, and will be perfectly ventilated by a system of fans run by power. The amphitheatre will be provided with all necessary lavatories, dressing-rooms, etc."

According to Haines, the building was designed to serve as many different people and functions as possible. "At the northwest corner of Madison Avenue and Twenty-seventh Street will be the theatre, perfect in all its appointments, fireproof in every respect, with a tenting capacity of 1,200, and containing all the latest stage improvements. At the right of the central entrance of the amphitheatre, facing on Madison Avenue and Twenty-seventh street, will be the cafe!, 30 by 50 feet, and the restaurant, 52 by 82 foot. On the second floor, approached through the tower by elevators and a staircase 10 feet wide, will be a concert-hall, 80 by 90 feet, exclusive of the stage, which will, with its galleries, be between 1,200 and 1,500 people. By the side of this concert-hall on Twenty-sixth street and opening into it will ho a small hall, 30 by 30 feet. Both the larger and smaller halls are connected by pantries with the service of the restaurant kitchen, and are intended to be used for large dinners. Balls may also be given in the larger hall, when the smaller will be used for a supper-room. This large hall will also at times be connected with the amphitheatre by a stairway, and used as a supper-room when largo balls are given in the amphitheatre. Over the smaller hall, reached from the tower, will be two room 20x30 feet, with lavatories adjoining, which will be used as dressing rooms in connection with the large hall or as private dining room in connection with the restaurant. The kitchen will be at the top of the building. The entire roof at the Madison Avenue end, 112 by 200 feet, will be available for a Hummer garden. The architects of the building are McKim, Mead & White, and the builder David H. King. Jr. The amphitheatre will he completed March 20, 1890, the theatre and music hall June 1, and the entire building, including the tower, Aug. 1."

When it was completed in June 1890, the second Madison Square Garden exceeded everyone's hopes and predictions. As Curtis put it, "Architecturally, it was a magnificent structure, simply styled in the Renaissance manner, of buff-colored brick and terra cotta. The flat roof was broken by a series of colonnades, cupolas, domes and a magnificent tower derived from the Giralda in Seville, surmounted by St. Gaudens' figure of Diana. Half way around the building was an open arcade supported by massive pillars of polished granite. The only elaborately decorative feature of the building was a relief arch in terra cotta above the main entrance."

Pictures of the exterior and interior of Madison Square Garden in the early 20ᵗʰ century

Curtis described the last few moments leading up to the opening of the second Madison Square Garden: "For weeks a night and day shift have been alternating at work around the building and everywhere there is a restless and curious excitement. The great Eduard Strauss of Vienna has been induced to journey here for the opening and present the music which his family has made immortal. Every seat and inch of standing room has been sold for days in advance of the opening — this is to be not only a great music festival, but the debut, as well, of New York's great acquisition, Madison Square Garden, now to be proudly flaunted along with Central Park, Brooklyn Bridge, and the new Aqueduct. As early as seven o'clock the line for standing room has been forming and at eight-thirty, one can trace its zig-zag course half around the block. It is shortly after eight and the surge of elegantes has commenced, arriving in open Victorias and broughams, with the liveried footman and coachman presiding over as a Cowboy the stable's prize span. The audience, in entirety, is in full dress and as one glances over the vast panorama, it seems to be but a series of rising, undulating, billowy coiffures, expressed by an array of puffs and pompadours, aigrettes and plumes, curls and combs. There is an apparent craning of necks and uncontrollable wonderment at the spectacle of this colossal structure around which one can scarcely see. Decorated throughout in a delicate tint, it seems to make one even more conscious of the great, unlimited space."

Once the dignitaries attending the opening arrived, they were treated to a show that was likely among the best they would ever witness. Curtis continued, "As I just overheard one reporter remark: 'It is a unique experience to sit with thousands of people under one roof, listening to the music of an orchestra two blocks away, and yet beneath this same roof.' The only spot of color is provided in the costumes of the ushers, with tawny orange breeches and flaming red waistcoats. The view of the auditorium is really enchanting. Before the regular tiers of seats and boxes begin, there are several hundred people sitting about at little tables, chatting with friends and newly made acquaintances. Upon a circular platform in the middle of the hall the orchestra has just appeared and now a slender, pensive — nay, almost worried-looking young man darts to the fore of the stage and with a wave of his baton, the orchestra blares forth the first few bars of the 'Beautiful Blue Danube.' There is thunderous applause, so deafening that Herr Strauss is forced to turn and bowingly acknowledge it before he continues. In another moment the famous Strauss dance music starts anew with this picturesque leader who has more nearly approached the ideal waltz tempo than any contemporary conductor. How he bends about like a willow, now stroking a few bars on his own violin, now drawing fantastic waltz pictures in the air with his fiddle bow, all of the while keeping his feet in motion under the intoxicating spell of his own music. A hushed awe has come over the audience as the vibrating mood and rhythm of the music penetrates its depths. It is quite apparent that they have but little interest in anything save the Strauss music and it is equally obvious that the orchestra renders it infinitely better than any we have ever been privileged to hear before."

Halfway through the program, the guests at the Garden were treated to something that many of them did not expect. In fact, it is unlikely that even those who had heard the amazing feature they were about to witness in action were ready for what they saw. Lewis explained, "It is intermission and before the ballets appear, I can observe some of the notables in the audience. But now everyone is gazing overhead, for the great glass roof is slowly sliding aside and we are sitting beneath a blue-black sky set with a sparkling field of stars. We are refreshed by such a gentle cool breeze as we sit here enjoying the advantages of outdoors and the comforts of the indoors. This, indeed, is an ideal place to spend a warm evening — everywhere around me I hear the safety, the convenience, the completeness, and perhaps most of all, upon the comfortableness of the place. A charming, beautiful house of entertainment. Quite some few of the audience who were interested only in Strauss are taking an early leave, while the rest are gradually finding their seats before the ballet begins. The first ballet has presented in pantomime 'Choosing the National Flower' followed by 'War and Peace,' a rather brilliant and animated spectacle, handsomely costumed, but still the anti-climax of the evening. Although the applause seems generous and spontaneous enough, the audience is manifesting a readiness to leave and after only four minutes have elapsed, the Auditorium is entirely empty. I see a large crowd congregating on the sidewalk and out into the street across at the Fifth Avenue Hotel and the resounding cry is 'Bravo !',

'Strauss !',' 'Strauss !' Presently the doors leading to a low balcony open and Herr Strauss, accompanied by his wife and daughter, appears. An impromptu serenade is struck up by a group of Italian hand organs, audible only during a lull in the cheering. Strauss is visibly overcome and at a loss to express his appreciation as he frequently turns to his family for the strength of their support. This has been the climax of an altogether great evening and is something for New Yorkers to talk of for weeks to come. The precedent is established and future events cannot escape a criticism in comparative terms."

The opening did indeed set a precedent. Lewis added, "During the first week of May in the year 1892, Madison Square Garden was selected as the only fitting place in which to stage the Actor's Fund Fair. The entire floor was laid out as a miniature village with models of famous theatres of ancient London and older New York brought into close proximity." Apparently, those attending this lavish production "might step from the Old Curiosity Shop into the Chatham Square Theatre of early New York, cross the street to the house of Shakespeare and from there move a few steps to the Globe Theatre and Dukes' Theatre of London. The opening night was marked by an attendance of practically 10,000 people, all viewing for a point of vantage from which to hear Joseph Jefferson, who had promised to act as Master of Ceremonies, and to see Edwin Booth, then in the hey-day of his career. For one week, here reigned a pandemonium of frantic selling and enthusiastic buying. True it is that bargains were made but trinkets were auctioned off at ten times their worth. This, too, marked the day of greater abandon, the time when one might manifest outward indications of joy or sorrow, the day before it was considered smartly fashionable to maintain a blasé nonchalance at the sight of anything. Today our enthusiasm is more conservatively created and more sparingly scattered. Not so in the early '90's when Adelina Patti sang here to three of the largest audiences ever assembled for concerts. When the Patti Farewell Festival was held, the immense Auditorium was packed to the doors with throngs of devout music-lovers who remained silently enthralled throughout the performance. But when Patti bade her formal adieu from the stage, there was a vast sweeping surge of the multitudes toward the platform, a last valiant attempt to counteract the 'goodbye forever,' and her managers were forced to intercede and carry her from the melee. And so through the years, Madison Square Garden has embodied the joys and shrouded the tragedies of a great people. Here new records were made and veteran champions dethroned."

Tragically, one of the "champions dethroned," in an altogether shocking manner, was Stanford White himself. On a warm evening in late June 1906, millionaire Harry K. Thaw, who had by this time married Nesbit, approached White while he watched the show *Mam'zelle Champagne* in the roof garden theater on top of Madison Square Garden. Pulling out a pistol, he shot White three times in the head. At first, those in the theater thought it was a prank, but when the smoked cleared and White's wound became visible, they knew they had just witnessed something horrific.

Thaw

The following months were little better, as Thaw stood trial in both the press and the courts. Stanford White's son would later complain, "On the night of June 25th, 1906, while attending a performance at Madison Square Garden, Stanford White was shot from behind [by] a crazed profligate whose great wealth was used to besmirch his victim's memory during the series of notorious trials that ensued." Eventually, Thaw was declared innocent by reason of insanity and sentenced to time in a mental hospital, and in the meantime, White's reputation was thoroughly disgraced, leading *Collier's* magazine to counter, "Since his death White has been described as a satyr. To answer this by saying that he was a great architect is not to answer at all…what is more important is that he was a most kindhearted, most considerate, gentle and manly man, who could no more have done the things attributed to him than he could have roasted a baby on a spit. Big in mind and in body, he was incapable of little meanness. He admired a beautiful woman as he admired every other beautiful thing God has given us; and his delight over one was as keen, as boyish, as grateful over any others."

Despite the murder of White and one of the 20th century's first cases to be billed as the "Trial of the Century," this Madison Square Garden continued to play host to just about every kind of event, as Curtis noted: "Madison Square Garden was the supreme court of the people, with the public as a jury of selection. Here, one might have his chicken, his dog, his horse, or his cattle, proclaimed the blue ribbon winner. Here there were contests of brain as well as brawn — the ringing oratory of a William Jennings Bryan, the superhuman hitting power of a Jack Dempsey. Here the people of a great city gathered to hear the war-time address of Woodrow Wilson and answered the call to muster arms. Here one might demonstrate his prowess as a cake-walker or a diva; a Paderewski or a Patti. That history repeats itself, there is no doubt. Madison Square Garden has come and gone, and a new structure replaces it. Madison Square used to be thought of as up-town and now, relatively speaking, it is down-town." -

Looking back on the second Madison Square Garden, *New York Telegraph* reporter Sam Taub once wrote, "Madison Square Garden, that has gone and the new one that has arisen to take its place, holds a spot in the heart of every New Yorker as no other institution does. It would hardly be fair to classify it as merely being a Gotham playground. It's scope is national and, from the interest aroused in sporting events and other affairs staged within its portals, the eyes of the entire world will always be focused on it. Memories of the old Garden will always linger; the arena on Madison Avenue, where the fans seemed frozen stiff the night Richie Mitchell knocked Champion Benny Leonard down in the sensational first round of their great bout in 1921 and where Jack Delaney three years later figured in his great victory over Champion Paul Berlenbach. The fans all have hopes of witnessing great ring battles and other notable events in the beautiful structure which has supplanted the old playhouse. The New Madison Square Garden is a lasting monument to our fair city and speaks volumes for the success of Promoter Tex Rickard, whose activities preserved the old arena for several years longer than the owners had wished."

The interior of the Garden in 1907

Chapter 3: A Veritable Palace of Sport

"Parting with an old friend is one of the saddest experiences that falls to the lot of man. Making a new friend is something over which one may rejoice exceedingly. That tells, for myself and other lovers of sports, the story of the passing of the old Garden and the birth of the new. Every stick and stone of the old Garden, now but a memory, was steeped in sporting lore. Champions were made and broken there. Many a human drama was enacted there before the eyes of tense thousands. But I shall leave it to others to tell of these things. The new Garden, a veritable palace of sport, is certain to be the foremost indoor arena of the world. It marks the progress of sport in a very substantial way. Thrilling scenes will be enacted there in the years to come. The new Garden stands as a monument to the promotorial genius of Tex Rickard. So did the old Garden, for that matter, as it was not until Rickard took charge there that the old Garden became what it should have been from the start. With the world's greatest promoter at the head of the world's greatest arena, Father Knickerbocker may look forward with every confidence to wonderful years in sport." - Wilbur Wood, reporter for *The New York Sun*

As wonderful as the second Madison square Garden was, it also eventually outlived its usefulness and faced replacement. In January 1925, one newspaper reported, "Tex Rickard announced today that active work in constructing his new Madison Square Garden in the heart of the White Way district, will begin on Monday and that if plans do not miscarry it will be open to the public on October 15 of this year. The building and outlay for the plot, 200 feet wide and 500 feet long, with entail $5,500,000."

Rickard

Apparently the groundbreaking itself was quite a show, as another paper reported, You can't appreciate how fast an elephant -walks until you see it on a crowded-street. Two circus elephants were sent to Eighth Avenue and Fiftieth Street to participate in the ceremony of breaking ground for the new Madison Square Garden. Children who followed had to run at top speed. The elephants kept pace with taxicabs. When they stopped at a cross street one of them put his trunk in a taxi window and a woman fainted."

In May, another paper mourned the end of the second Madison Square Garden: "Madison Square Garden for three decades the scene of big sporting events and public assemblages has sung its swan song. A turbulent throng of 13,000 last night watched Sid Terris, youthful New

York light weight, outpoint the veteran Johnny Dundee in the building's farewell athletic event. The statue of Diana atop the Garden tower will be lowered today as wreckers begin to tear down the structure to make way for an office building. A new Madison Square Garden will be built by Tex Rickard several score blocks from Madison Square. ... The Garden treated New York to many a thrill. Among the knights of the roped arena who traded punches under its roof were Sullivan, Fitzsimmons, Gans, Corbett, Mitchell, Sharkey, Jeanette, Donovan, Dixon, Langford, Cross and Attell as well as the later day crop of Leonard, Britton, Wills, Dempsey, Firpo, Walker, Jackson and Dundee. The songs of Patti had echoed from its walls, and into its distant corridors had rung the speech of William Jennings Bryan, Theodore Roosevelt and Woodrow Wilson. Here were given annually for years the horse show, the circus and the six-day bicycle races. It was in the Garden that Stanford White, its architect, was shot and killed by Harry K. Thaw. It was in the Garden that the democratic convention broke the record for deadlocks and Alabama and its votes for Underwood became famous."

At the same time, there were many who both mourned the loss of the old Garden and praised the new one. Paul Gallico of the *New York News* wrote, "They carted away bricks and rubbish and slabs of stone and twisted steel, I suppose, thinking if they stopped to do so, that they were tearing down Madison Square Garden. The task they did was, in a way, absurdly incomplete. The old Garden still stands. No one has attempted to seek out and destroy those who knew and loved that spot. Memory must be obliterated and those who inhabited the famous pile must mingle with the dust of its crumbled cement before it can be said to have passed. Tex Rickard now has a grand, new, shiny place where everything he had before will be bigger and better. I suppose the thing to do will be to forget the old Garden in the splendors of the new. Will it be the same? Will it be different? Who can tell? But I suspect it will be a long long time before the old Garden is destroyed from the memory and traditions of Old New York."

In evaluating the new Garden, J.A. Sessler, its Works Manager, asserted, "If the story of the New Madison Square Garden is a Twentieth Century version of Aladdin's Lamp for modern science, engineering and mechanical skill have been invoked prodigiously in the construction of the present structure, the third to bear the name made famous by its predecessors. The present Garden is the conception of the two master showmen, Mr. George L. Rickard and Mr. John Ringling. In its appointments as to both safety and comfort for its patrons, it is the last word in engineering skill. The cost of the project was approximately $5,000,000. The building extends from 49th to 50th Street, 125 feet west of Eighth Avenue, and is 375 feet long. It was designed by the well-known theatre architect, Thomas W. Lamb, with James Stewart & Company, Inc., as contractors. Thirteen entrances are distributed at both sides of the building and also on Eighth Avenue. Altogether 350 lineal feet of exits are so arranged that the entire building can be cleared in five minutes."

Sessler went on to tell the story of its construction: "Ground was broken on the 16th of February, 1925, and the building completed nine months later to the day. To accomplish this remarkable constructive feat, it was necessary to consider the size of the operation — the largest of its kind ever undertaken; the limited time at our disposal; the varied nature of the work, and the engineering skill necessary. With these rigorous requirements in mind, contractors were selected as to their ability to expeditiously execute their work and to cooperate with the owner and each other on the entire installation. It is a pleasure to give testimony to the fact that the various contractors…not only cooperated with the owners, their co-workers and other contractors, but executed their work with the utmost efficiency. The main auditorium is most impressive, being 200 feet wide and 375 feet long and affords unobstructed view for 19,000 persons for whom accommodations are provided. The arena floor proper is 110 feet wide by 240 feet long. Not a single column is used in the main arena, the immense roof being carried on trusses spanning from 49th to 50th Street, weighing 60 tons each, which, together with the 3,400 tons of steel members in the structure, were installed by Taylor-Fichter Steel Construction Company. The Exposition Hall, located under the auditorium, has a clear space of 52,000 square feet available for entertainments or exhibitions. An automatic sprinkler system is provided throughout. Water, power, light and gas connections are located at each pier and pilaster. In addition to the ventilating system…special provision has been made to accommodate exhibitors requiring an exhaust system for the gasses from oil-burning apparatus or internal combustion engines."

Sessler also made it clear that while the Garden was most associated with sporting events, the new Garden was designed to be used for a variety of purposes. "The Arena and that portion of the Exposition Hall devoted to dancing, together, provide the largest dance floor area on the continent — 55,000 square feet. These floors are of pink Tennessee, highly polished terrazzo which, when properly prepared, provide an ideal floor for dancing. The building is strictly fireproof throughout, and does not contain a single piece of lumber. It is unquestionably the world's greatest exhibition forum. One of the outstanding features of the new Arena will be the ice hockey and skating rink. With a skating surface of 186x85 feet the world's greatest hockey teams and fastest skaters will use the rink for National and International contests of speed and skill. The most scientific and modern freezing plant has been installed, including twelve miles of piping, and an ice surface one inch thick can be provided in eight hours and removed in six. The magnitude of the task is shown by the flexibility required in a three-day section of the new arena schedule which calls for boxing on Friday, December 18; hockey play on Saturday, December 19, and a grand concert on Sunday, December 20. The ventilation and the air conditioning system was designed to cope with a number of different conditions which present themselves; when the building is used for hockey, during which time the ventilation must be controlled in spite of the large ice surface; boxing matches, at which time the auditorium affords a maximum seating capacity; bicycle races, when the auditorium will be occupied continuously for six days; circuses, when animal odors must be eliminated; as well as conventions during summer and winter; cinametograph and operatic performances, and dancing."

A postcard depicting the new Madison Square Garden

A picture of the new Garden

Chapter 4: The Crowning Achievement

"As one marvels at the magnificence the new Madison Square Garden unfolds — there never was anything to compare with this arena dedicated to sports in this or any other country — he pauses to ponder what the future holds for the crowning achievement of Tex Rickard's notable promotorial career. Rickard does things on a big scale. Naturally one visualizes the greatest line of sporting events New York, and that means America, ever has known. Already a higher standard has been set for the six-day bicycle race. Boxing should take another forward step under the refining influence of this new setting and hockey regain the popularity it once enjoyed in the time of the immortal Hobey Baker. Eventually, too, the National Horse Show will be sheltered in the new temple of sport and when it is it will step out on the tanbark as in the halcyon days of twenty or twenty- five years ago." - Len Wooster, Sports Editor for the *Brooklyn Daily Times*

As impressive as the architecture of the new building was, what really made it special in the eyes of 1920s America was its comfort, particularly as it related to controlling the quality and temperature of the environment in which the patrons would be seated. Sessler described amazing improvements in the facility's ventilation system: "The functioning of the ventilating system is assisted by the employment of ozonizers, air washers and filters which will deodorize the air, removing dust and dirt particles as well as the smoke. Ventilation is of the utmost importance as health insurance to our patrons which is assured for the arena ventilating system consists of a combined outside and recirculated air supply which provide a minimum of 400,000 cubic feet of filtered and ozonized air per minute; equaling 21 cubic feet of air per minute per person. This very liberal supply of air is delivered by eight large fans located in the attic space, each having a capacity of 50,000 cubic feet of air per minute. The air, after being filtered and ozonized, can be either recirculated into the building through the eight supply fan rooms, or exhausted from the building by other fans. The ventilating system of the Exposition Hall will provide at least six complete changes of air per hour. Here again there is a combined outside and recirculated air supply, with air filters, dehumidifiers and ozonizers, so that the atmosphere in the large show room is under the same excellent conditions of control as that in the arena. Ventilating systems entirely separate from the main ventilating units have been provided for all the kitchens, toilets and rest rooms throughout the building."

Sessler also talked about the way in which the building could be kept warm in the winter and cool in the summer. "In order that the temperature in all portions of the building might be constantly under manual as well as automatic control, there have been installed control rooms on the arena floor and in the Exposition Hall. At twenty-four points in the arena and at fifteen points in the Exposition Hall are located temperature recording instruments. These instruments are such that the temperature at other points of location is recorded in the control rooms. From these control rooms also, the speed of the motors driving the fans, the dampers controlling the fresh and the recirculating air, can all be controlled. There are five 225 H.P. Fitzgibbons high-pressure boilers, feed water heater, duplicate vacuum return pumps and boiler feed pumps, as well as a vacuum ash removal system which eliminates all the handling of ashes inside the building. The boilers supply steam to the three 300 H.P. turbines driving the refrigerating machinery. The low-pressure exhaust steam from these turbines or steam direct from the boilers to pressure reducing valves is led to the many units of Aerofin heaters and the radiators throughout the building. The condensed steam from these heaters and radiators is returned to the boilers by the vacuum method. In addition to the manual control of the temperature and humidity previously described, the temperature in all parts of the building will be automatically controlled and maintained at any predetermined degree between 65 and 70 regardless of the outside temperature, except when the building is being used for ice skating or hockey games, when a lower temperature will be maintained. The heating and ventilating system as designed by Dwight D. Kimball and installed by E. G. Woolfolk & Company, both of New York City."

Although the common use of air conditioning in private homes was still a couple of generations away, the 1925 Madison Square Garden did have some interesting climate control features. Sessler explained, "All that has been said of ventilation is especially true of cooling during the summer season. The temperature in the auditorium will be ten degrees lower than the outside temperature at any time during the summer. In order to accomplish this, the Carrier Engineering Corporation, the leading specialists in the field of air conditioning, installed a special system to cool the air and to reduce the humidity. This reduction in humidity is just as important as a reduction in temperature. In this case, however, the dehumidification is produced by drawing the air through finely atomized sprays of refrigerated water. The temperature of this water is sufficiently low to cause condensation of the moisture in the air. The quantity of this relatively dry, cold air which is delivered to the auditorium is so regulated that when mixed with a supply of warmer air, ideal conditions of physical comfort are produced. After passing over the audience, the air is drawn through a multitude of registers, whence it is taken to be re-purified and re-cooled, or is discharged out of doors. Refrigeration has been introduced, not only to cool the water for the spray chambers, where the air is cooled, but to freeze the water with which the entire floor of the area is flooded when the ice rink is in operation. This portion of the work was designed by the Funk and Wilcox Co., engineers, Boston, Mass. The freezing of the water is accomplished by circulating brine at a low temperature through some twelve miles of pipe imbedded in the arena floor. For these combined uses, a set of three centrifugal refrigeration machines was installed. These refrigeration machines are unique in that they operate under conditions of vacuum, and the possibility of outward leaks and obnoxious odors to the building is entirely eliminated. The refrigerant is a harmless liquid, known as 'Dieline' and offers no hazard whatever to the occupants of a public building. This was a very important consideration in selecting refrigeration equipment for a building such as the Garden. To summarize regarding ventilation, no expense has been spared in providing this new civic monument with the facilities for maintaining, at all seasons of the year and on all occasions, the ideal condition of temperature, humidity and air purity for the health-giving physical comfort of the thousands of spectators and performers who will assemble in this building."

Of course, while spectators enjoyed being comfortable, they came to the Garden to see something special, and that was always what was most important. In order to enjoy whichever event they had purchased tickets for, they had to be able to hear what was going on and see what was happening. According to Sessler, this concern was also on the minds of those designing the building. "The Western Electric 'Public Address System,' which has been installed will distribute sound, uniformly and clearly over the entire auditorium. Until the advent of the Public Address System it had been practically impossible in large auditoriums and convention halls for the voice to reach all parts with equal intensity. Practically all parts of the building are linked by means of a system of automatic intercommunicating telephones, which is almost indispensable to the efficient operation of a building of such vast proportions. The power and lighting requirements of the building are served by two direct current and by two alternating current supplies. The lighting for the arena is on a balanced 3-wire 1 10-220 volt direct current distributing system. The Exposition Hall lighting is 1 10 volts alternating current. All motor circuits in the building are 220 volts direct current, while two and three phase power is available for exhibition purposes. Main switchboards with necessary circuit breakers, meters, etc., are located in the basement on each of the current supply systems. From these boards the current is fed to the various panel boxes throughout the building. Special readily accessible panels have been installed to control the exit lighting circuits which are normally fed by direct current. There has been installed a transfer switch which instantly and automatically cuts the exit circuits over into alternating current, should the direct current supply fail. When the direct current supply is resumed, the circuits are instantly cut back."

   Although the 1920s were a time of social and technological advances, people attending a big event in a crowded arena likely thought of the various horror stories about fiery disasters that had claimed so many lives in the past. Sessler mentioned this concern as well: "For the protection of the public as well as the building, there has been installed the National District Telegraph Company's watchman and fire-alarm signal-box service, with twenty-five stations throughout the building; and the Holmes Electric Protective Service for the protection of the box offices." Then, having addressed every concern he could think a patron might have, he concluded his remarks by mentioning a couple of the "perks" unique to the new Garden. "Restaurants are located in the building adjacent to the Exposition Hall and club rooms, for the accommodation of patrons. The executive offices are located alongside 49th Street on the first floor. The Club Room, whose members comprise the best known sportsmen of New York, is located on the 50th Street side."

Picture of a 1937 rally against Nazi Germany in the Garden

CONTESTANT 44

ARENA SECRETARY

Tex Rickard presents – The Third Annual

WORLD SERIES RODEO

October 23 to November 1, 1928

Madison Square Garden

New York City

Morgan Evans

SIGNATURE OF CONTESTANT

A chit for the World Series Rodeo at the Garden in 1928

Chapter 5: Madison Square Garden IV

"1968 advertisement showing architect's model of the final plan for the Madison Square Garden Center complex. The neighborhood is known as Pennsylvania Plaza. The original Pennsylvania Station in New York City, located on the site where Madison Square Garden sits today. On February 11, 1968 Madison Square Garden IV opened after the Pennsylvania Railroad tore down Pennsylvania Station (New York City) and continued railway traffic underneath. The new structure was one of the first of its kind to be built above an active railroad system. It was an engineering feat constructed by R.E. McKee of El Paso, Texas. Public outcry over the demolished Beaux-Arts structure led to the creation of the New York City Landmarks Preservation Commission. The current Garden is the hub of Madison Square Garden Center in the office and entertainment complex formally addressed as Pennsylvania Plaza and commonly known as "Penn Plaza" for the railroad station atop which the complex is located." – An excerpt from http://www.nyc-architecture.com

As soon as it opened in the fall of 1925, the new Madison Square Garden was quickly subjected to reviews, which included plenty of criticism. Joe Vila, a Sports Editor with *The Sun*, wrote, "The passing of Madison Square Garden is mourned by followers of sport. It is only natural that the demolition of this landmark of sport, where so many famous boxing bouts and other sport events took place should arouse keen regret. Yet the fact that there is a new Garden, a bigger and better Garden and one that will outdo the old in the matter of sports, more than makes up for this regret. As a devotee of sports for more than 30 years I have many happy recollections of the old Garden. Still, I do not hesitate to say that the new structure represents a vast improvement over the old. The Garden was rather a 'white elephant' until Tex Rickard took charge there in 1920. Had not Rickard stepped in when he did, the old Garden probably would have been razed several years ago. Rickard's success with the old Garden was such as to guarantee that he will make the new amphitheatre what it was designed to be, the greatest temple of sport in the world."

Nat Fleischer, a sports editor for the *New York Telegram*, praised the new arena: "All hail to Madison Square Garden, the greatest boxing center in the world. All hail to the genius— Tex Rickard — who conceived the idea of building a sports arena of such gigantic proportions, an arena which stands forth as a monument to the sport of ages — boxing! Boxing was at its lowest level when Rickard came forth from the West to announce to a gathering of reporters in the Biltmore that he had visions of making Madison Square Garden a CENTRE of AMERICA'S SPORTS ACTIVITIES, and that he had leased the Garden for ten years in order that he might develop this vision into a reality. That he succeeded despite obstacles which would have forced persons with less grit, less determination and fighting spirit to go under, is a credit to this man's wonderful ability in the showman's game, the ability of a master artist in the field of promotion. Tex Rickard has gained his just reward in the form of a great monument — the Madison Square Garden."

It goes without saying that all of the four buildings carrying the name of Madison Square Garden saw their fair share of life, but what many forget is that the Garden also played host to death. Besides the murder of Stanford White, Benny Paret fell into a coma after a 1962 boxing match against Emile Griffith, and Paret died 10 days later. Writing about this event decades later, Johnathan Coleman, who witnessed the event as a child, recalled "the cold, blustery Saturday evening of March 24, 1962, when I happened to be at Madison Square Garden. I was ten and a half years old, a fifth-grade student at a boarding school in Maryland, and I was attending the Griffith-Benny 'Kid' Paret fight for the world welterweight championship…. This was the first big prize fight I had ever seen in person, and I loved everything about it: the smell of cigar smoke, the palpable tension surrounding a big event, and the growing buzz of the crowd in anticipation of what was to come, as one fight after another on the undercard concluded, all leading to the main event. There was the dramatic ping-ping of flashbulbs popping, and the silence that befell the huge arena as everyone waited for the fighters to make their way down their respective aisles, toward the elevated ring and its plush ropes. All of it felt irrecoverably, deeply primal, though I feel pretty sure that, at the time, I didn't know what 'primal' meant. But I would soon find out."

Coleman remembered, "The fight was a slugfest, and Paret nearly ended things in the sixth round. But after six more rounds, things ended for Paret as Griffith punched him senseless against the ropes, sending him into a coma from which he never emerged. He died ten days later. Norman Mailer, who was also in attendance that night in a ringside seat, wrote, 'As he took those eighteen punches something happened to everyone who was in psychic range of the event. Some part of his death reached out to us. … As he went down, the sound of Griffith's punches echoed in the mind like a heavy axe in the distance chopping into a wet log.' Mailer summed things up with the following words: 'Paret died on his feet.' Mailer was right. Some part of Benny Paret's death did reach out to all of us. I had not witnessed death before, and what I remember most clearly was the hushed silence in the arena as Paret was moved, ever so carefully, from the floor of the ring onto the stretcher, beginning a procession down the aisle of the Garden where I was sitting and where, as it turned out, Angus was, too. (His seat, however, was closer to the ring; he always had ringside seats because, as he later explained, 'I knew everybody.') It might as well have been a funeral procession without a casket. When the stretcher approached where we were seated, I looked—not for long, but long enough to see Paret's battered face and the blood on his white satin trunks. That image, that instant, bore itself permanently into my memory."

Paret's death seems to have tinged the third Madison Square Garden with a certain feeling of danger or perhaps gloom, for only a few years passed before rumors began to circulate that it should be replaced with a newer, more up-to-date building.

This time, however, it would be at a new and, it was hoped, better location. Irving Felt purchased the rights to build above the original Pennsylvania Railroad, but the decision was not without controversy since it would involve tearing down the beautiful and popular Pennsylvania Station and most of the above ground portions of the railroad. In November 1963, papers across the country carried a photo with the following caption: "PENNSYLVANIA STATION BOWS TO TIME — A two-ton stone eagle is lowered from the side of Pennsylvania Station in New York as demolition is started. On hand to picket were five architects who had battled to save the station because they considered it a classic example of early 20th century eclectic American style. Present at the demolition…were: J. Benton Jones of the Pennsylvania Railroad; Irving Felt of the Madison Square Garden Corp., and Thomas Goodfellow of the Long Island Railroad. The station will be replaced by a new Madison Square Garden sports arena and a 33-story office building built over the railroad complex in the future."

Penn Station in 1963 before being torn down

Ultimately, people adjusted to the changes, and in February 1966, Arnie Burdick wrote the following in the *Syracuse Herald American*: "It's a vastly different architectural face that Manhattan Island presents to its visitors these days, and probably the most breathtaking change is occurring right above old Penn Station. There, bounded by 31st and 33rd Streets and Seventh and Eighth Avenues, rises the new Madison Square Garden. This is a magnificent $315 million sports and business complex that many believe will come to be known as the 'Ninth Wonder of the World.' (Houston's Astrodome being accepted recently as the eighth, at least by the Sports Colony.) 'We're progressing extremely well,' Fred Podesta told us just the other day. Podesta, a veteran Garden officer, was just named President of the new MSG Attractions, Inc. 'As of now, we are right on target to open as planned in the fall of '67,' he went on. 'Naturally, that's subject to the weather. And materials. But as of now, we're on target.'"

Obviously, building on top of a former railroad station offered unique challenges, as Burdick was quick to point out: "The most difficult phase of the construction—covering over the station—has already been completed. The steel now stretches five-six floors above ground, and 'the work should now proceed very quickly.' The actual construction of the new Garden involves complicated engineering on a scale never attempted In New York, for-the work goes on without interfering with the 850 trains and some 250,000 people who use Penn Station daily. The present

Garden, about 20 blocks to the North on Eighth Avenue, was opened in 1925, and though it has undergone a series of modernizations, face-liftings and other improvements, in no way can it be compared with the new Garden that will supplant it."

In the end, Burdick agreed with others that it was worth it, noting:

> "MSG's home of the future will be a many-splendored thing. A 29-slory office building is being constructed adjacent to the circular complex, which will be a 13-slory doughnut containing the following:
>
> - The Forum, seating 5,000 for sports, theatrical productions, conventions, meetings.
> - The Exposition Rotunda, the size of two football fields for trade and consumer shows, will have 100,000 square feet available.
> - The Cinema, a 500 seat theater completely equipped for small meetings, closed-circuit TV showings, etc.
> - A 48-lane bowling house.
> - A Gallery of Art which will house the home of the National Art Museum of Sport and the MSG Hall of Fame. "

And, of course, the new Garden had more than 28,000 seats without a girder or pillar blocking anyone's view. "'The biggest difference in the new Garden,' enthused Podesta, 'is that we'll have 51 percent more good seats. All of the seats will be in the main circle. There'll be no balcony (5,800 of the current Garden's 18,000 seats are in the balcony). It'll be comparable to one big mezzanine.' In building the new multi-level exhibition and sports complex of the future, Garden officials seem to have thought of just about everything. It'll be completely air-conditioned, naturally, and It will also be interlaced with a wide variety of restaurants and shops. Too, it will contain a 21-berth truck dock to eliminate costly waiting by those who have lo load or unload materials for shows and exhibits. Lighting will be superb and infinitely brighter than the old Garden. Parking, one of today's major headaches for promoters, will be taken care of by the '6,004 available spaces that are right in the area,' feels Podesta. 'We have built-in parking, for our peak loads will come during the evening, when the businessmen of the area are away from their offices. The two buildings will occupy only about half of the 8 ½ Acres of land available on the site, with the rest of the area being reserved for beautifully landscaped walks and plazas. No longer will there be a soiled 'Jacobs Beach' running alongside the MSG of the future. Believe me, it'll be a new Garden —both inside and out!" ("Jacob's Beach" was the nickname for the boxing ring at the Garden).

The Garden under construction

The recently completed Garden in 1968

Chapter 6: The Garden's Stage

"The building housing Madison Square Garden IV was developed on the full block between 31st and 33rd Streets and Seventh and Eighth Avenues and opened on February 11, 1968, over the underground Penn Station. The original Pennsylvania Station, a majestic building similar to Grand Central Terminal, had been torn down under the excuse of it being too costly to maintain. Its developers were given a complete real estate tax pass by then-Mayor Ed Koch, who later realized the actual legislation had no sunset date, an issue that to this day ruffles city administrations and plagues the Garden ownership. Garden IV was built around its core moneymakers: the three-ring circus, Rangers ice hockey and Knicks basketball, but has hosted both Democratic and Republican Conventions and other events from monster trucks to bull-riding, show jumping and a youth rally with then-newly elected Pope John Paul II on Oct. 2, 1979. While the cover of Rolling Stone may be a highlight of a rock act's career, performing at Madison Square Garden is the pinnacle of worldwide touring. Nearly every popular performer has played the Garden's stage. … Now, with its modern renovation and technology, the Garden is now poised and ready to continue to host history-making moments well into the future." – Lois Rice, journalist

As predicted, the new Garden opened to significant fanfare on February 8, 1968. A United Press International Article raved, "P. T. Barnum, who opened the first Madison Square Garden in 1874 to house his circus, would have only one word for the fourth and newest Madison Square Garden-'Jumbo!' Everything's jumbo about the $150 million garden which will be opened by Bob Hope in a show business extravaganza Sunday night before an audience which paid as much as $250 a ticket to attend the historic occasion. The new garden is part of Madison Square Center, the world's largest complex for sports expositions, conventions, and entertainment. It has more escalators, a bigger air purifying system, longer steel beams, more dressing rooms and the most extensive interior roadway (dubbed 'the elephant walk') of any entertainment-sports palace in America. Furthermore it is the only such building constructed without federal, state or city aid—a landmark monument to private enterprise. Madison Square Garden Corp. stock is listed on the big board at nearly $12 a share, up seven points from its 1967 low. Unlike the old Madison Square Garden, which had only two money-making facilities, the new garden has seven areas of activity including the 20,000- seat main arena, a 5,227 seat amphitheater, a 64,000 square foot exhibition rotunda, a 501- seat cinema, a 48-lane bowling alley, a garden hall of fame, and the national museum of sports. Investors expect it to be a money-maker. Led By Bob Hope, The United Service Organizations (USO) has raised $1 million on seat sales for the Sunday benefit premiere titled 'The Night of a Century,' starring Hope, Bing Crosby, Pearl Bailey, Barbara Eden, Les Brown and a host of entertainment stars. The show will be taped by NBC-TV and televised nationally at 9:00 p.m. EST next Monday. The bowling alleys and amphitheater have been open since November, but workmen are still completing some areas of the complex. The center and its adjoining 29-story glass office tower have been under construction for two years on the site of Pennsylvania Station, which is now located below ground on the two block site on Eighth-Avenue."

As the author of the article was quick to point out, part of the new Garden's attraction was its location. "The Garden has the advantage of sitting astride a subway-bus-train hub connecting New York and the suburbs. It is clean, colorful, comfortable, spacious, and designed for quick access and exit—none of which attributes could describe die old Madison Square Garden, which, in consequence, lost its female patrons in droves in recent years. 'We determined to bring back the Missus and all the kids,' said a Garden official. 'We've even got girl guides and hostesses, just like the airlines.' Every seat in the Garden is upholstered in warm spectrum colors and the 404-foot diameter suspended dome, which precludes any sight obstructions in the arena, is as gay as a gigantic roulette wheel, with cream and orange spokes. Gone are spotlights which glare, amplifiers that echo, and floor seams that were a hazard for hockey stars and ice ballerinas."

Of course, the real attraction for the new Garden, just as it was for the predecessors, was the entertainment, and the article promised the best was to come: "The Garden will play' host to traditional events such as the National Horse Show, Westminster Kennel Club Show, National Invitational Basketball Tournament, New York Ranger Hockey, prizefights, Ringling Bros. Circus, and Israel bond rallies. It has already attracted new events, including the U.S. Lawn Tennis Association's International Tournament and the Professional Bowlers Association tournament. The amphitheater, named for Garden President Irving Mitchell Felt, will attract a whole new range of entertainment as well as forums and conventions. Stitch Henderson holds the spotlight currently as conductor of a series of concerts with the American Symphony Orchestra. The next booking is Jane Morgan and the Doodletown Pipers. The Hall of Fame will mount exhibitions recalling the history of the garden, which has echoed to the speeches of every president since Grover Cleveland, to the voices of great singers since Adelina Patti and die thud of Boxing gloves since John L. Sullivan. The museum will display works of art pertaining to sport, beginning with Rembrandt's 'The Sport of Golf,' and will commission contemporary artists to continue die tradition."

The article concluded by praising the building itself: "The Charles Luckman-designed Garden, a round windowless concrete structure with pebbly outer surface, is a tremendous improvement on the barn-like old Madison Square Garden, but it is inoffensibly undistinguished. It certainly lacks the airy charm of Stanford White's Moorish-towered pavilion that succeeded Barnum's Garden on the original Madison Square site from 1890 to 1925. But the garden provides New York, at long last, with a facility that can house such gatherings as major political conventions. The last Presidential convention in New York was at Madison Square Garden in 1924 when the Democrats nominated John W. Davis. Garden officials are counting on luring one of the parties here in 1972 to write another colorful chapter of the arena's long history."

One of the finest features in the new Garden was its music hall. Writing for United Press International, Frederick Winship proclaimed, "One of the most attractive features of the new Garden was its concert hall, which was designed in part by famed conductor Leopold Stokowski. In speaking about his work a few days before the location opened, he observed, 'When a concert hall is built, the first consideration should be acoustics. Sometimes an architect makes his plans and then when the hall is built, he begins to think about acoustics. It is not a good plan.'" The article added, 'To fit the sleek new hall—also built for staging of athletic events—to his music, Stokowski called for the addition of wood paneling behind and to the side of the portable stage, and baffling overhead. The baffling will be tilted and re-tilted until it brings forth just the sound Stokowski seeks from his bass and cello section, which has been placed at the rear of the stage."

Over the four decades that followed its opening in 1968, Madison Square Garden continued to host even more and better events than its predecessor had, and while it also suffered the same problems that the others experienced with the passing of time, those involved chose a better option than tearing it down. Instead, the Garden was given a renovation, and beginning in 2011, the Garden underwent a major overhaul that took two years to complete. Reporter Joe DeLessio believed the changes were worth it: "Madison Square Garden has undergone major renovations — or a 'transformation,' to use their preferred word — over each of the past three summers. The finished product will be unveiled to the public tomorrow night, when the Knicks take on the Bobcats in a preseason game, but officials showed off the building's new look earlier today. The Seventh Avenue entrance was totally redone this summer. The arena doors are now located at the top of these steps, in front of the entrance to the theater. (Previously, the doors were located closer to the box office.) Beyond those doors is an area called Chase Square, which is more open than this space was pre-renovation. On both the north and south sides of Chase Square, just beyond the arena doors, there's a video board built into the ceiling. The new, larger center-hung scoreboard. ...at first glance it appears to be a big improvement over the old scoreboard. Smaller screens are built into the bottom of the scoreboard for fans with seats near the ice or court — and for the players themselves to look at, if necessary."

While the Garden has been used for a number of large meetings and rallies, as well as huge concerts, it is still best known as a sports arena, and it was that aspect of its use that DeLessio was most interested in: "All the Rangers banners are grouped together on the Seventh Avenue side of the arena. ... There's also a second LED ribbon board on both the Seventh Avenue and Eighth Avenue ends of the arena. ... The Garden added ten more 'Defining Moments' displays in the concourses this year. This one commemorates the Rangers' 1994 Stanley Cup title. (That's the jersey Craig MacTavish was wearing when he took the final face-off in game seven of the finals.) Other new displays include Larry Johnson's four-point play in 1999, and Syracuse's six-overtime win over UConn in the 2009 Big East Tournament. The view from the northern Chase Bridge. We only spent a few seconds in these seats during the tour, but when facing the court, it didn't feel drastically different than sitting in the front row of the upper level in any other arena. (The major difference is that, instead of looking over a railing, you're looking through a pane of glass, similar to the design of the West Balcony seats installed last year.)"

One major change in the new Garden was the addition of bridges that would allow fans to get from one side of the building to the other without having to go all the way around the place. While some welcomed the increased convenience these bridges offered, others were concerned about the effect they would have on fans' views of the events. DeLessio continued, "Our biggest concern about the bridges is that they'd obstruct the views of the seats in the back rows of the main seating bowl. But the views from these seats weren't as bad as we expected. …though the main scoreboard is blocked, it doesn't feel as cramped as we feared. (There are smaller video boards built onto the back of the bridges.) The real test will be whether fans walking along the bridge will be a distraction during an actual game. For what it's worth, Garden officials insist it won't be. Today's tour didn't include a visit to the blue seats on the Eighth Avenue side of the building, though Hank Ratner, CEO of the Madison Square Garden Company, said that there are no obstructed views there, even in the back rows. The new capacity for hockey will be 18,006; for basketball, it'll be 19,812. That hockey capacity is roughly 200 seats fewer than the pre-renovation number of 18,200, though a Garden spokesperson says the actual capacity has been fluctuating in recent years, so the building hadn't necessarily held that many for Rangers games in recent seasons."

Following the completion of the renovations, the Garden entered a new phase in its life when famed singer Billy Joel announced he would be holding regular concerts there. A December 2013 article in *Rolling Stone* reported, "In an unprecedented move, Billy Joel announced at a New York press conference this afternoon that he will play Madison Square Garden once a month for the indefinite future. 'Playing Madison Square Garden is an experience that never gets old,' Joel said. 'A show a month at the Garden for as long as there's demand means more opportunities to connect with music fans and provides a unique and memorable show every time we play here.' After he spoke, MSG officials unveiled a new Billy Joel MSG logo next to ones for the Knicks, the Rangers and the Liberty. 'Billy, having you as our music franchise feels a little like having the Pope as your parish priest,' said MSG Executive Chairman James Dolan. 'I'm truly an admirer and I grew up with your music, too, and so I'm thrilled to death.' The residency kicks off January 27th, 2014 and continues with additional shows on February 3rd, March 21st, April 18th and May 9th. It's unclear when additional shows will be announced, and there is no end date to the residency. Officials at the press conference reiterated they would continue 'as long as there is demand.' Single-artist residences have been a Las Vegas staple for decades…. This is the first time, however, that a major artist has announced such an endeavor outside of Las Vegas. The once-a-month scheduling is also a historic first."

A modern picture of the Garden

Online Resources

The Most Famous Landmarks of New York City: The History of the Brooklyn Bridge, Statue of Liberty, Central Park, Grand Central Terminal, Chrysler Building and Empire State Building by Charles River Editors

Bibliography

Anderson, Dave (February 19, 1981). "Sports of the Times; Dues for the City". The New York Times.

Bagli, Charles V. (September 12, 2005). "Madison Square Garden's Owners Are in Talks to Replace It, a Block West". The New York Times.

Huff, Richard (August 22, 2006). "Arena's the Star of MSG Revamp". Daily News (New York).

Printed in Great Britain
by Amazon